glamour

AT HOME

15 timeless designs to knit and keep forever

ERIKA KNIGHT
COLLECTABLES

photography by Katya de Grunwald

Quadrille

Editorial director Jane O'Shea
Creative director Helen Lewis
Designer Claire Peters
Project editor Lisa Pendreigh
Editorial assistant Andrew Bayliss
Pattern checker Rosy Tucker
Photographer Katya de Grunwald
Photographer's assistant Amy Gwatkin
Stylist Beth Dadswell
Illustrator Bridget Bodoano
Pattern illustrator Anthony Duke
Production director Vincent Smith
Production controller Bridget Fish

First published in 2007 by
Quadrille Publishing Limited
Alhambra House
27–31 Charing Cross Road
London WC2H 0LS
www.quadrille.co.uk

Text and project designs
© 2007 Erika Knight
Photography
© 2007 Katya de Grunwald
Design and layout
© 2007 Quadrille Publishing Limited

British Library Cataloguing-in-Publication
Data: a catalogue record for this book is
available from the British Library.

ISBN 978 184400 510 9

Printed and bound in China

GLAMOUR
AT HOME

introduction

Glamour at Home is a decorative collection of knitted pieces designed to add a little extravagance to everyday interiors. Each design is created with decadence in mind, from sumptuous cushions in silk, satin-like cotton, whisper-fine mohair or ornate jacquard to a vintage-inspired throw with Oriental patterning and knitted lace; as well as a whimsical tea cosy, silver sequinned lampshade and rose-scented sachets. The yarns are sensuous, soft and pretty, in a palette of pearl pink, antique rose, amethyst, Lalique green, teal, petticoat peach, soft gold and lacquer black. The stitches are simple yet lavishly married with sumptuous fabrics, prints and patterns, and the details add more than a touch of luxury with ribbons, tassels, beads, sequins and pussycat bows.

glamour home collection

the
patterns

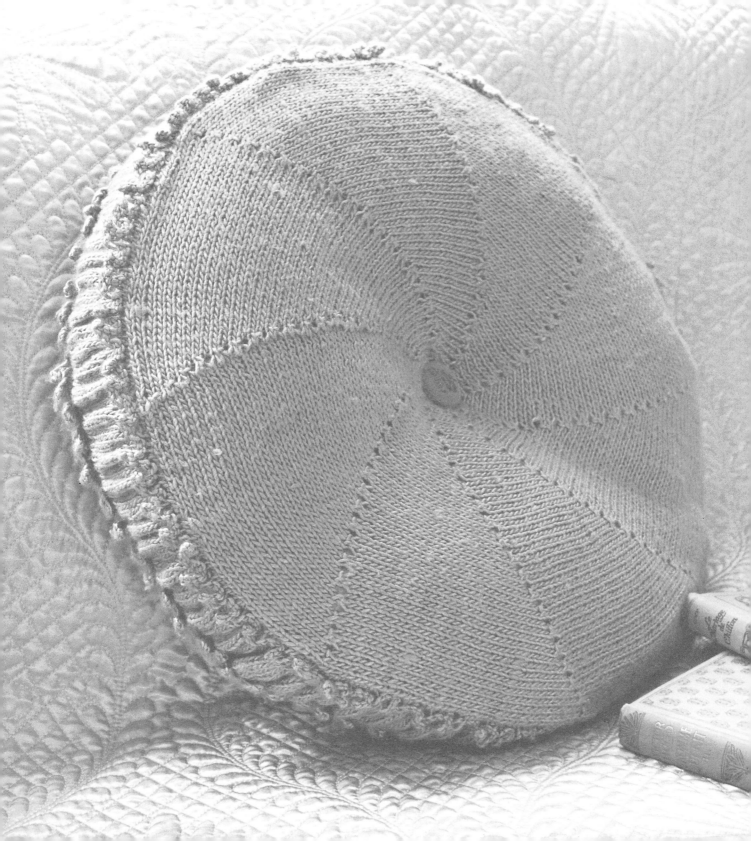

round ruched cushion

Made in a pure silk yarn in the prettiest of soft greens, this cushion is a beautiful accessory for any couch or bed. The round cushion shape is achieved using easy short-row shapings, which are simple but so effective. The border is worked in a frivolous ruched stitch edged with little picots, while the front and back are both finished with a covered button that enhances the vintage character.

materials

Any double-knitting-weight yarn, such as Debbie Bliss *Pure Silk*
  4 x 50g hanks
Pair of 4mm knitting needles
3.75mm circular knitting needle
Large blunt-ended yarn needle
38cm round cushion pad with gusset
2 large buttons to cover
Scrap of silk fabric or ribbon to cover buttons

size

One size, approximately 40cm in diameter

tension

24 sts and 32 rows to 10cm over stocking stitch using 4mm needles

pattern notes

- For the short-row shaping, when the instructions say 'turn' at the end of the row, this means that the remaining stitches are not worked. In order to avoid creating a hole when turning on a knit row, work a wrap stitch – knit as far as instructed, then slip the next stitch purlwise onto the right-hand needle, bring the yarn forward between the two needles, slip the stitch back to the left-hand needle and take the yarn to the back between the two needles, turn and purl to the end of the next row.
- Keep precious yarns, such as silk, in a pillowslip while you work to avoid pilling.

To make cushion front

Using 4mm needles, cast on 44 sts.
Work in st st and short rows as foll:
Row 1: K all sts.
Row 2: P all sts.
Row 3: K to last 2 sts, turn (see Pattern Notes).
Row 4: P.
Row 5: K to last 4 sts, turn.
Row 6: P.
Cont working in short rows as set, leaving 2 more sts unworked on every knit row until there are no more sts to knit.
This completes the first segment of circle.
Start again with row 1 and cont until 8 segments have been worked to form a full circle.
Do not cast off sts, but join last segment to first segment by grafting one st from needle with corresponding st on cast-on edge.

To make cushion back

Work exactly as for cushion front.

To make ruched gusset

Using 3.75mm circular needle, work picot cast-on edging as foll:
*Cast on 6 sts onto left needle using knit-on cast-on method, cast off 3 sts, slip st left on right needle onto left needle; rep from * until 276 sts have been cast on onto left needle.
Beg with a k row, work 4 rows in st st, ending with RS facing for next row.
Next row (RS): K1, *k into front and back of next st; rep from * to last st, k1.
Beg with a p row, work 6 rows in st st, ending with WS facing for next row.
Next row (WS): P1, *p2tog; rep from * to last st, p1.
Beg with a k row, work 4 rows in st st, ending with RS facing for next row.
Work a picot cast-off edge as foll: *Cast off 6 sts, slip st left on right needle onto left needle, cast on 3 sts; rep from * to end.

To finish

Weave in any loose yarn ends.
Lay front and back out flat and gently steam. (Do not steam ruched gusset.)
Sew together row ends of ruched gusset to form a circle.
The gusset is sewn to cushion leaving picot edgings free.
To make it easier to sew on, measure gusset, then divide into eight equal sections and mark them with a pin. Pin each section on one side of gusset to a segment of cushion front and sew gusset to front.
Sew gusset to cushion back in same way, leaving an opening for inserting cushon pad. Insert cushion pad and sew opening closed.
Cover buttons with silk fabric. Position one button at centre of each side of cushion and sew them together, stitching through cushion and pulling thread tightly to indent centre of cushion.

boudoir lampshade

Slip this opulent lacy cover over your
paper lampshade to add a touch of
feminine glamour to a bedside table or
dresser. Knitted in mercerised cotton,
it is made up of six segments, three in
Turkish stitch and three in diamond
stitch, and has a pretty edging at the
top and bottom. The finished cover is
embellished with matt and shiny sequins
along with glass beads to gently shimmer.

materials

Any super-fine-weight mercerised cotton yarn, such as
    Yeoman *Cotton Cannele 4ply*
    1 x 250g cone
Pair of 3.25mm, 4mm and 5.5mm knitting needles
Medium-size blunt-ended yarn needle
Approximately 100 small silver matt sequins
Approximately 20 small silver shiny sequins
Approximately 220 small clear glass seed beads
Approximately 50 small clear glass bugle beads
Sewing needle and sewing thread for sewing on beads
Lampshade, approximately 72cm around lower edge, 36cm around
    upper edge and 17cm tall

size

One size, approximately 17cm tall

tension

Turkish stitch: 10 sts to 6cm over pattern using 4mm needles
Diamond stitch: 12 sts to 6cm over pattern using 4mm needles

To make Turkish stitch panels (make 3)

With 5.5mm needles, cast on 10 sts.
Work 2 rows in garter st (k every row).
Patt row 1: K2, *yfwd, sl 1, k1, psso; rep from * to last 2 sts, k2.
Rep last row 6 times more.
Next row (inc row): K into front and back of first st, k1, *yfwd, sl 1, k1, psso; rep from * to last 2 sts, k into front and back of next st, k1.
Cont in patt as set **and at the same time** inc 1 st as before at each end of 4 foll 6th rows. *20 sts.*
Work straight in patt for 4 rows.
Work 2 rows in garter st.
Cast off knitwise.

To make diamond stitch panels (make 3)

Using 4mm needles, cast on 11 sts.
Work 2 rows in garter st.
Row 1 (RS): P2, k2tog [k1, yfwd] twice, k1, sl 1, k1, psso, p2.

Row 2 and every foll WS row: K2, p7, k2.
Row 3: P2, k2tog, yfwd, k3, yfwd, sl 1, k1, psso, p2.
Row 5: P2, k1, yfwd, sl 1, k1, psso, k1, k2tog, yfwd, k1, p2.
Row 7: P2, k2, yfwd, sl 1, k2tog, psso, yfwd, k2, p2.
Row 8: As row 2.
Rep last 8 rows to form diamond stitch patt **and at the same time** inc 1 st at each end of next row and then at each end of every foll 4th row until there are 27 sts, taking inc sts into st st.
Cont in patt until row 8 of 5th diamond stitch patt repeat is complete.
Work 2 rows in garter st.
Cast off knitwise.

Edging

Using 3.25mm needles, cast on 6 sts.
Row 1 (WS): K1, k2tog, yfwd, k2, [yfwd] twice, k1. *8 sts.*
Row 2: K1, [k1 tbl] twice into double yfwd, k2tog, yfwd, k3.
Row 3: K1, k2tog, yfwd, k5.
Row 4: Cast off 2 sts, k2tog, yfwd, k3. *6 sts.*
Rep last 4 rows until work fits around lower edge of shade.
Cast off.
Rep on upper edge of shade.

To finish

Weave in any loose yarn ends.
Pin out six panels and gently steam.
Lay panels side by side, alternating stitch patterns, and graft them together.
Grafting loosely to maintain lace effect, join straight edge of edgings to upper and lower edges.
Sew sequins and beads randomly to main panels and stitch beads to lower edging.

jacquard bolster

This substantial bolster cushion is made up of square patches – in both lacy knit stitches and decorative fabrics. Each end of the cushion is finished with a circle knitted using a simple short-row shaping technique and decorated with a chunky tassel and button detail.

materials

Any super-fine-weight cotton yarns, such as:

A: small amount of Jaeger *Siena* in green)
B: small amount of Rowan *Cotton Glacé* in ochre
C: small amount of Yeoman *Cotton Cannele 4ply* in beige
D: 1 x 250g cone of Yeoman *Cotton Cannele 4ply* in brown
E: small amount of Yeoman *Cotton Cannele 4ply* in grey

Approximately 30cm in each of four fabrics:

F: chinoiserie fabric in grey/black
G: silk fabric in green
H: silk jacquard in gold/aqua
I: silk dupion in taupe

Pair of 3.25mm knitting needles
Medium-size blunt-ended yarn needle
45cm long x 17cm in diameter feather-filled bolster pad
17 large mother-of-pearl buttons, 2cm in diameter
24 small mother-of-pearl buttons, 1.5cm in diameter
Microfilament sewing thread
Black Staflex for backing patches

size

One size, approximately 45cm long x 17cm in diameter

tension

Each knitted square measures 15cm by 15cm using 3.25mm needles

pattern note

- For the short-row shaping, when the instructions say 'turn' at the end of the row, this means that the remaining stitches are not worked. In order to avoid creating a hole when turning on a knit row, work a wrap stitch – knit as far as instructed, then slip the next stitch purlwise onto the right-hand needle, bring the yarn forward between the two needles, slip the stitch back to the left-hand needle and take the yarn to the back between the two needles, turn and purl to the end of the next row.

special abbreviations

Cr2L = pass right needle behind first st on left needle and k 2nd st tbl, then k first st and slip both sts off left needle.

Cr2R = pass right needle in front of first st on left needle and p 2nd st, then p first st and slip both sts off left needle.

To make circular ends for bolster (make 2)
Using 3.25mm needles and D, cast on 20 sts.
Work in garter st and short rows as foll:
Row 1: K all sts.
Row 2: K all sts.
Row 3: K to last 2 sts, turn (see Pattern Note).
Row 4: K.
Row 5: K to last 4 sts, turn.
Row 6: K.
Cont working in short rows as set, leaving 2 more sts unworked on every alternate knit row until there are no more sts to knit.
This completes the first segment of circle.
Start again with row 1 and cont until 12 segments have been worked to form a full circle.
Do not cast off sts, but join last segment to first segment by grafting one st from needle with corresponding st on cast-on edge.

To make tassels (make 2)
Wrap a generous amount of each colour yarn used around a piece of cardboard 12cm by 25cm.
Wrap a length of yarn a few times around strands at one end of cardboard and knot, leaving long enough loose ends for stitching tassel in place.
Cut strands at other end of tassel (see page 97).
Wrap another length of yarn around tassel, approximately 2.5cm from top, linking and securing ends under wrapping.
Make a second tassel in same way.

Checks and cords square
Using 3.25mm needles and C, cast on 34 sts.
Row 1 (RS): K1, *k4, p2, Cr2L,

p2; rep from * to last st, k1.

Row 2: P1, *k2, Cr2R, k2, p4; rep from * to last st, p1.

Rows 3–6: Rep rows 1 and 2 twice.

Row 7: K1, *p1, Cr2L, p2, k4, p1; rep from * to last st, k1.

Row 8: P1, *k1, p4, k2, Cr2R, k1; rep from * to last st, p1.

Rows 9–12: Rep rows 7 and 8 twice.

Rep last 12 rows until square measures 15cm. Cast off.

Blackberry stitch squares (make 3)

Using 3.25mm needles and A, cast on 34 sts.

Row 1 (RS): K1, *[k1, yfwd, k1] into next st, p3; rep from * to last st, k1.

Row 2: P1, *p3tog, k3; rep from * to last st, p1.

Row 3: K1, *p3, [k1, yfwd, k1] into next st; rep from * to last st, k1.

Row 4: P1, *k3, p3tog; rep from * to last st, p1.

Rep last 4 rows until square measures 15cm. Cast off.

Using D, make two more squares in same way.

Cobnut stitch squares (make 2)

Using 3.25mm needles and B, cast on 32 sts.

Row 1 (RS): *P3, [k1, yfwd, k1] into next st; rep from * to end.

Rows 2 and 3: *P3, k3; rep from * to end.

Row 4: *P3tog, k3; rep from * to end.

Row 5: P.

Row 6: K.

Row 7: *P1, [k1, yfwd, k1] into next st, p2; rep from * to end.

Row 8: K2, *p3, k3; rep from * to last 4 sts, p3, k1.

Row 9: P1, *k3, p3; rep from * to last 5 sts, k3, p2.

Row 10: K2, *p3tog, k3; rep from * to last 4 sts, p3tog, k1.

Row 11: P.

Row 12: K.

Rep last 12 rows until square measures 15cm. Cast off.

Using E, make one more square in same way.

To finish

Weave in any loose yarn ends on knitted squares.

Lay squares out flat and gently steam.

Backing piece

For backing piece for bolster cover, cut a piece of Staflex, 71cm by 45cm.

Fabric patches

Cut a template for square fabric patches, 15cm by 15cm plus 1.5cm all around for seam allowance. Using template, cut the two complete squares, six half squares and four quarter squares shown on diagram opposite, allowing 5cm extra along buttonhole and button band edges at top and bottom.

Patchwork arrangement

Iron fabric patches onto backing, then machine zigzag stitch around edges, using microfilament thread. Zigzag stitch knitted squares in place over seam allowances of fabric patches.

Button decoration

Sew one large button to centre of each of six knitted squares, then sew four small buttons around each of these as shown.

Using seven large buttons, sew one to each corner of two square fabric patches at centre of patchwork.

Bolster assembly

Turn under 5cm at top and bottom of patchwork and stitch.

Make two buttonholes evenly spaced on centre patch of one end. Overlap buttonhole end over button band end and topstitch for approximately 10cm at each end to secure. Sew on two large buttons to correspond with buttonholes.

Cut out two circles of fabric, each the size of bolster end plus 1.5cm seam allowance all around. Turn patchwork cover wrong-side out and pin and stitch fabric ends in place.

Turn right-side out and hand stitch knitted bolster ends in place.

Sew a tassel to centre of each end of bolster, stitching it in place through a large button.

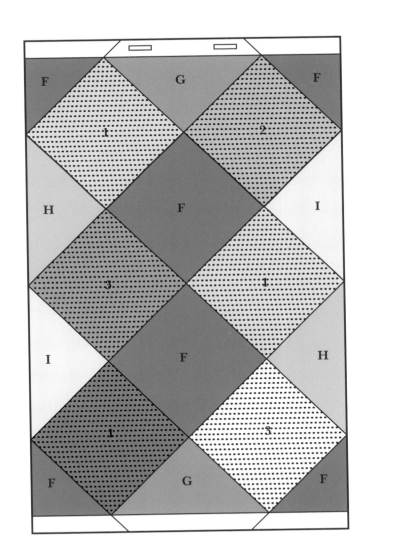

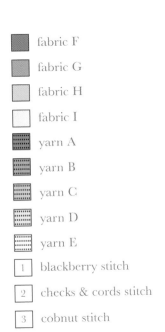

fabric F

fabric G

fabric H

fabric I

yarn A

yarn B

yarn C

yarn D

yarn E

1   blackberry stitch

2   checks & cords stitch

3   cobnut stitch

poochy pouffe

What every pampered pet needs – a gorgeous cushion to sit on and look adorable. Knitted in basic stocking stitch, the animal-print motif can either be knitted in or embroidered on to the cushion. The main yarn is a luxurious cotton, but wool blends would work just as well. Along with a simple twisted braid and four tassels, a glittery knitted corsage ensures your pet is 'Best in Show'.

materials

Any medium-weight cotton or wool-blend yarn, such as
  Rowan *RYC Luxury Cotton DK*
  A: 6 x 50g balls in dark brown
  B: 3 x 50g balls in off-white
Any super-fine-weight metallic yarn, such as Rowan *Lurex Shimmer*
  C: 1 x 25g ball in black
  D: 2 x 25g balls in white gold
  E: 1 x 25g ball in bronze
Pair each of 3.25mm and 4mm knitting needles
Pair each of 3.25mm and 3.75mm double-pointed knitting needles
Large blunt-ended yarn needle
4 wooden beads, 2cm in diameter, for tassels
30cm of black satin ribbon, 2.5cm wide, for rosette
Large sew-on jewel or button
Sewing needle and sewing thread for stitching rosette
3 large press fasteners
40cm x 60cm feather-filled cushion pad

size

One size, approximately 40cm x 60cm

tension

22 sts and 30 rows to 10cm over stocking stitch using B and
  4mm needles

pattern notes

- If you prefer to embroider the colour pattern onto the knitting, follow the instructions for the embroidered top.
- When working the stocking stitch colour pattern from the chart, read odd-numbered rows (knit rows) from right to left and even-numbered rows (purl rows) from left to right.
- Work the colour pattern using the intarsia technique, using a separate ball (or long length) of yarn for each area of colour and twisting yarns on wrong side of work where colours change to avoid holes forming.

To make cushion base pieces (make 2)
Using 4mm needles and A, cast on 132 sts.
Rib row 1: *K1, p1, rep from * to end.
Rep last row until work measures 3.5cm from cast-on edge, ending with RS facing for next row.
Beg with a k row, work 25cm in st st.
Cast off.

To make cushion top
Using 4mm needles and B, cast on 132 sts.
Embroidered top only:
Beg with a k row, work 40cm in st st.
Top with knit-in pattern only:
Beg with a k row, work 2 rows in

st st, ending with RS facing for next row.
Beg with a k row and chart row 1, work 75 rows following chart, ending with WS facing for next row.
Beg with a p row and using B only, cont in st st until work measures 40cm from cast-on edge.
Both versions:
Cast off.

To make edging cords (make 2)
Using a pair of 3.25mm double-pointed needles and one strand of D, cast on 6 sts.
Row 1 (RS): K.
Row 2 (RS): Without turning right needle, slide sts to right end of right needle and transfer this needle to left hand, take yarn across WS of work from left to right and pull

tightly, then k to end.
Rep last row until work measures approximately 2m.
Slip sts onto a st holder and do not break off yarn.
Using a pair of 3.75mm double-pointed needles and A, cast on 5 sts and make second cord in same way as first cord.

To make rosette circles (make 2)
Using 4mm needles and A, cast on 28 sts.
Beg with a k row, work 2 rows in st st, ending with RS facing for next row.
Shape as foll:
Row 1 (RS): *K1, k into front and back of next st; rep from * to end.
Row 2 and every foll WS row: P.

Row 3: *K2, k into front and back of next st; rep from * to end.
Row 5: *K3, k into front and back of next st; rep from * to end.
Row 7: *K4, k into front and back of next st; rep from * to end.
Row 9: *K5, k into front and back of next st; rep from * to end.
Row 11: *K6, k into front and back of next st; rep from * to end.
Row 12: As row 2.
Cast off.
Using 3.25mm needles and one strand of D, make second rosette circle in same way.

To make tassels (make 4)
Cut a generous number of lengths of A, D and E, each approximately 30cm long.
With lengths aligned, tie a strand of D around centre.
Place a wooden bead in centre of strands and fold them around bead.
Then wrap a length of D around

'neck' of tassel below bead. Keep winding to make a little band, then tie tightly.
Trim tassel.
Make three more tassels in same way.

To finish
Weave in any loose yarn ends.
Lay top and base pieces out flat and gently steam.
Embroidery
If embroidering colour pattern, follow chart using Swiss darning and gently steam again.
Cushion seams
Overlap two base pieces at ribbed edge to form a rectangle 60cm by 40cm.
Then sew base to cushion top, using mattress stitch.
Edging cord
Twist two cords around each other and pin around edge of cushion.
Adjust cord lengths if necessary

and cast off.
Sew twisted cord in place.
Rosettes
Sew row-end edges together on each rosette circle. Then work running stitch around cast-on edge of each circle, pull to gather and secure end.
Place circle in D on top of circle in A and join together by stitching a large button or jewel through centre.
Fold ribbon into a V-shape and sew to bottom of rosette as shown. Sew finished rosette to cushion top as shown.
Tassels
Sew a tassel to each corner of cushion.
Sew three press fasteners evenly spaced to overlapped rib edges of cushion base.
Insert cushion pad.
Call for pup or puss!

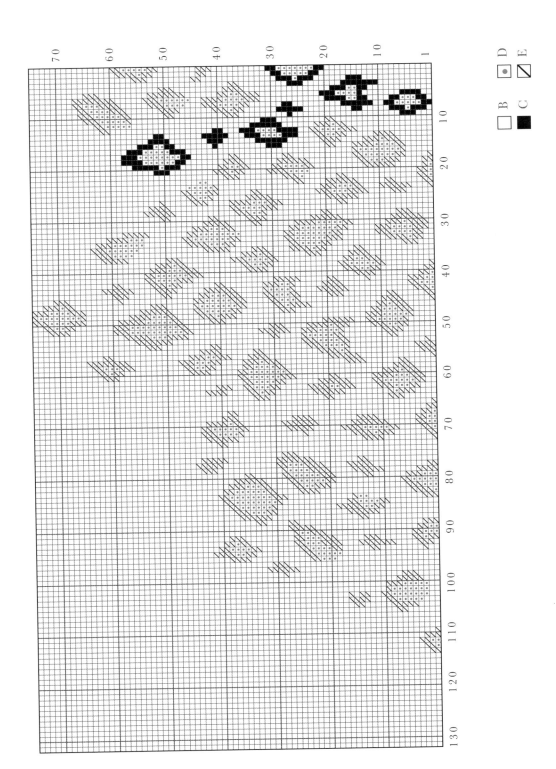

ornate slippers

These pretty slippers are made in vibrant mercerised cotton. Knitted in basic stocking stitch, with the yarn used double, the simple fully-fashioned shaping ensures a great fit and subtle detailing. Each slipper is embellished with fashionable grosgrain ribbon and a selection of tonal jewels for a stylish result.

materials

Any super-fine-weight mercerised cotton yarn, such as
    Yeoman *Cotton Cannele 4ply*
    1 x 250g cone in aubergine
Pair of 4mm knitting needles
Large blunt-ended yarn needle
33cm of grosgrain ribbon, 4cm wide
1m of satin ribbon, 1.5cm wide
8 large square faceted sew-on jewels
2 small square faceted sew-on jewels
2 small round faceted sew-on jewels
Sewing needle and sewing thread for sewing on jewels

sizes

Size	small	medium	large	
Finished length	18.5	19.5	20.5	cm

Note: Slippers stretch to fit so that they fit snuggly.

tension

22 sts and 28 rows to 10cm over stocking stitch using yarn double
    and 4mm needles

pattern note

•   The yarn is used double throughout.

To make right sole

Using 4mm needles and yarn double, cast on 5 sts.

Shape heel end

Work sole in st st as foll:

Row (RS): K.

Row 2: P1, m1, p to last st, m1, p1.

Row 3: K1, m1, k to last st, m1, k1.

Rep last 2 rows once more. *13 sts.*

Work straight until sole measures 10.5 (11.5: 12.5)cm, ending with RS facing for next row.

Shape toe end

Next row (inc row) (RS): K2, m1, k to end.

Next row: P.

Rep last 2 rows 1 (3: 5) times more. *15 (17: 19) sts.*

Work straight until sole measures 18.5 (19.5: 20.5)cm from cast-on edge, ending with RS facing for next row.

Next row (RS): K2, k2tog, k to last 4 sts, k2tog tbl, k2.

Next row: P.

Rep last 2 rows until 7 sts remain. Cast off.

To make left sole

Work as for right sole, but work toe-end inc rows as foll:

Inc row (RS): K to last 2 sts, m1, k2.

To make uppers (make 2)

Using 4mm needles and yarn double, cast on 6 sts.

Work upper in st st as foll:

Row 1 (WS): P.

Row 2: K2, m1, k to last 2 sts, m1, k2.

Row 3: P2, m1, p to last 2 sts, m1, p2.

Rep last 2 rows until there are 22 (26: 30) sts.

Next row: K2, m1, k to last 2 sts, m1, k2.

Next row: P.

Rep last 2 rows until there are 30 (32: 40) sts.

Work straight until upper measures 8 (9: 9.5)cm, ending with RS facing for next row.

Shape sides

Next row (RS): K14 (15: 19) and slip these sts onto a st holder, cast off next 2 sts, k to end.

Working on these 14 (15: 19) sts only, cont as foll:

Next row: P.

Next row: K3, k2tog, k to end.

Next row: P.

Rep last 2 rows until 11 (12: 16) sts remain.

Work straight until upper measures 18 (21: 23)cm from cast-on edge, ending with RS facing for next row.

Next row (RS): K2, m1, k to end.

Work straight for 3 rows.

Rep last 4 rows, twice more. *14 (15: 19) sts.*

Work straight until upper measures 21.5 (23: 24.5)cm from cast-on edge. Cast off.

With WS facing, rejoin yarn to sts on holder and p to end.

Next row (RS): K to last 5 sts, sl 1, k1, psso, k3.

Next row: P.

Rep last 2 rows until 11 (12: 16) sts remain.

Work straight until upper measures 18 (21: 23)cm from cast-on edge, ending with RS facing for next row.

Next row (RS): K to last 2 sts, m1, k2.

Work straight for 3 rows.

Rep last 4 rows, twice more. *14 (15: 19) sts.*

Work straight until upper measures 21.5 (23: 24.5)cm. Cast off.

To finish

Weave in any loose yarn ends.

Lay work out flat and gently steam.

Sew together cast-off edges of uppers with an outside seam to form heel.

With wrong sides together, pin sole to upper, easing to fit, and sew using mattress stitch.

Decoration

Cut grosgrain ribbon in half, fold ends in to centre to make a double thickness and press. Sew jewels to grosgrain ribbons as shown and sew to uppers.

Cut two 10cm lengths of satin ribbon. Fold under ends of each piece, then fold in half widthways to form a loop. Stitch one loop to centre back heel seam on each slipper.

Use remaining satin ribbon to tie slippers together when not in use.

pleated ruffle cushion

This cushion is predominantly made up of a pretty knitted ruched panel worked in a gorgeous silk yarn. A chinoiserie satin panel is stitched to one end to create a modern style patchwork cushion that is trimmed with a velvet ribbon and then embellished with a corsage of silk fabric and knitted petals. The back consists of a classic cotton floral print and a tonal silk fabric and is fastened with mother-of-pearl buttons.

materials

Any double-knitting-weight silk yarn, such as Debbie Bliss *Pure Silk*
    2 x 50g hanks
Pair of 4mm knitting needles
Medium-size blunt-ended yarn needle
Approximately 50cm in each of three different fabrics, such as:
    A: chinoiserie satin jacquard
    B: plain silk dupion
    C: cotton floral print
Approximately 50cm of velvet ribbon, 2cm wide
Matching sewing thread for stitching cover
3 mother-of-pearl buttons
30cm x 40cm feather-filled cushion pad

size

One size, approximately 30cm x 40cm

tension

24 sts and 32 rows to 10cm over stocking stitch using 4mm needles

To make pleated cushion front
Using 4mm needles, cast on 70 sts.
Beg with a k row, work 9 rows in st st,
ending with WS facing for next row.
Beg pleat patt as foll:
Row 1 (WS): P5, *[with right
needle, pick up loop of next st
7 rows below and place on left
needle, then p tog picked-up loop
and next st on left needle] 4 times,
p4; rep from * to last st, p1.
Rows 2–8: Work 7 rows st st, beg
with a k row.
Row 9 (WS): P1, [pick up loop and
p as before] 4 times, *p4, [pick up
loop and p] 4 times, rep from * to
last st, p1.
Rows 10–16: Work 7 rows st st,
beg with a k row.
Rep last 16 rows until work
measures 20cm from cast-on edge,
ending with RS facing for next row.
Beg with a k row, work in st st
until work measures 30cm from
cast-on edge.
Cast off.

Outer section of corsage
Using 4mm needles, cast on 14 sts.
Row 1: K into front and back of
each stitch. *28 sts.*
Row 2: *K2, m1; rep from * to last
2 sts, k2. *41 sts.*
Row 3: *Cast on 15 sts onto left
needle, cast off 17 sts, slip st on
right needle back onto left needle;
rep from * to end.

Inner section of corsage
Work as for outer section until end
of row 2.
Row 3: *Cast on 9 sts onto left
needle, cast off 11 sts, slip st on
right needle back onto left needle;
rep from * to end.

To finish
Weave in any loose ends of yarn.
Cushion front
Cut a piece of fabric A 33cm by
13cm and sew to cast-off edge of
knitted section, stitching close to
edge on knitting and taking a
1.5cm seam on fabric.
Using a zipper foot, sew velvet
ribbon over seam to cover it.
Cushion back
Cut a piece of fabric B 33cm by
32cm. To form a buttonhole band,
turn under 1.5cm and then 6cm
along one long edge and stitch.
Make three horizontal buttonholes
evenly spaced along band.
Cut a piece of fabric C 33cm by
31cm. To form button band, turn
under 1.5cm and then 5cm along
on one long edge and stitch.
Place buttonhole band section over
button band section so back pieces
are overlapping to create a cushion
back 43cm wide. Baste layers to
together to hold them in place.
With right sides of back and front
together, pin and baste, then sew all
around edge. Turn right-side out.
Sew on buttons.
Insert cushion pad.
Corsage
Cut two pieces of fabric C
approximately same size as knitted
corsage sections and cut them to
make a fringe.
Place fabric fringe pieces on top of
knitted fringe, pleat into a circle
and sew to secure.
Pin finished corsage to front of
cushion with a safety pin.

scented sachets

These scented sachets are made in beautiful fine silk, in two different stitch patterns, and worked with glass beads to create something exquisitely pretty and enduring. Each knitted square features a turned hem that is tied with satin ribbons to finish, and slipped inside is an organza envelope filled with a pot pourri of rose petals or lavender.

materials

Any super-fine-weight silk yarn, such as Jaeger *Silk 4ply*
    1 x 50g ball
Approximately 1300 beads, for scented pillow with all-over beads
Approximately 220 beads, for scented pillow with knots and beads
Pair of 3mm knitting needles
Medium-size blunt-ended yarn needle
Small piece of organza and matching sewing thread to make
    inner bag
Lavender or rose petals to fill inner bag
Satin ribbons

size

One size, approximately 12.5cm x 12.5cm

tension

Scented pillow with all over beads: 28 sts and 52 rows to 10cm over
    beaded stocking stitch using 3mm needles
Scented pillow with knots and beads: 28 sts and 40 rows to 10cm over
    beaded knot pattern using 3mm needles

pattern notes

• Before starting to knit, thread the beads onto the yarn. The
  simplest way to do this is to thread a sewing needle that will
  pass through the bead with sewing thread. Knot the ends of the
  thread and put the yarn through this loop. Thread a bead onto
  the needle and slide it along onto the yarn. Continue until all
  the beads have been threaded onto the yarn.

special abbreviations

bead 1 = bring yarn to front (**RS**) of work between two needles, slip bead up next to st just worked and slip next st purlwise from left needle to right needle to leave bead in front of slipped st, then take yarn to back (**WS**) of work between two needles.

make knot = p3tog leaving sts on left needle, then k same 3 sts tog, p them tog again and slip sts off left needle.

To make scented sachet with all-over beads

Using 3mm needles, cast on 42 sts. Beg with a k row, work 6 rows in st st, ending with RS facing for next row.

Next row (ridge row) (RS): P, to form foldline ridge.

Next row: P.

Now add beads where indicated as foll:

Row 1 (RS): K2, *bead 1, k1; rep from * to last 2 sts, k2.

Row 2: P.

Row 3: K3, *bead 1, k1; rep from * to last st, k1.

Row 4: P.

Rep last 4 rows until work measures 25cm from ridge row, ending with WS facing for next row.

Next row (ridge row) (WS): K, to form foldline ridge on RS.

Beg with a k row, work 6 rows in st st. Cast off.

To make scented sachet with knots and beads

Using 3mm needles, cast on 42 sts. Beg with a k row, work 6 rows in st st, ending with RS facing for next row.

Next row (ridge row) (RS): P, to form foldline ridge.

Next row: P.

Now make knots and add beads where indicated as foll:

Row 1 (RS): K1, *make knot, k3; rep from * to last 5 sts, make knot, k2.

Row 2: P.

Row 3: K2, *bead 1, k5; rep from * to last 4 sts, bead 1, k3.

Row 4: P.

Row 5: K4, *make knot, k3; rep from * to last 2 sts, k2.

Row 6: P.

Row 7: *K5, bead 1; rep from * to last 6 sts, k6.

Row 8: P.

Rep last 8 rows until work measures 25cm from ridge row, ending with WS facing for next row.

Next row (ridge row) (WS): K, to form foldline ridge on RS.

Beg with a k row, work 6 rows in st st. Cast off.

To finish both sachets

Weave in any loose yarn ends. Lay work out flat and gently steam on WS to avoid damaging beads. Fold in half widthways and sew both side seams. Turn top edge to inside along ridge row and sew in place. Sew a length of ribbon to each side of opening.

Inner bag

Cut a strip of organza 15.5cm by 29cm. Fold in half widthways and sew sides taking 1.5cm seams. Turn right-side out and fill with rose petals or lavender. Slip stitch opening closed. Insert bag into knitted cover.

chinoiserie throw

This lavish throw consists of seven fabric panels, four of which are pieced and have three sections of appliquéd lacy knits in each panel. The back of the throw is made up of larger fabric pieces, all with a vintage feel.

materials

Any super-fine-weight mercerised cotton yarn, such as
  Yeoman *Cotton Cannele 4ply*
  Small amount in four different colours – tangerine, dusty pink,
  light pink and light sage
Any double-knitting-weight silk yarn, such as Debbie Bliss *Pure Silk*
  1 x 50g hank in mauve
Pair of 4mm knitting needles
Assorted fabrics in five different colours (and matching thread) for
  patchwork, such as
  A: chinoiserie silk in three colourways
  B: floral print cotton lawn
  C: silk dupion
10 x 1m lengths of assorted velvet and satin ribbons and
  sequin strands
Staflex
Microfilament sewing thread

size

One size, approximately 127cm x 127cm

pattern notes

- Make 12 assorted knitted patches using the stitch patterns on the opposite page, in a variety of yarns and colours and introducing coloured stripes as desired.
- Make each patch either 24cm long or 24cm wide so they can be appliquéd in place either vertically or horizontally across a 24cm panel. (For vertical patches, work a swatch to determine how many stitches to cast on for a 24cm width.)

To make knit patches
Using 4mm needles, make 12 knitted patches (see Pattern Notes).

Cell stitch
Cast on a multiple of 4 sts plus 3 sts.
Row 1 (RS): K2, *yfwd, sl 1, k2tog, psso, yfwd, k1; rep from * to last st, k1.
Row 2: P.
Row 3: K1, k2 tog, yfwd, k1, *yfwd, sl 1, k2tog, psso, yfwd, k1; rep from * to last 3 sts, yfwd, sl 1, k1, psso, k1.
Rows 4 and 5: K.
Row 6: P.
Row 7: K.
Row 8: P.
Rep last 8 rows to form patt.

Van Dyke stitch
Cast on a multiple of 10 sts plus 1 st.
Row 1 (RS): K1, *yfwd, k3, sl 1, k2tog, psso, k3, yfwd, k1; rep from *.
Row 2 every WS row: Purl.
Row 3: K1, *k1, yfwd, k2, sl 1, k2tog, psso, k2, yfwd, k2; rep from *.
Row 5: K1, *k2, yfwd, k1, sl 1, k2tog, psso, k1, yfwd, k3; rep from *.
Row 7: K1, *k3, yfwd, sl 1, k2tog, psso, yfwd, k4; rep from *.
Row 8: As row 2.
Rep last 8 rows to form patt.

Little shell pattern
Cast on a multiple of 6 sts plus 2 sts.
Row 1 (RS): K.
Row 2: P.
Row 3: K2, *yfrn, p1, p3tog, yon, k2, rep from *.
Row 4: P.
Rep last 4 rows to form patt.

Undulating lacy rib
Cast on a multiple of 9 sts plus 2 sts.
Rows 1, 3, 5, 7 and 9: *K2, yfwd, k1, yfwd, k2, k2tog tbl, k2tog; rep from * to last 2 sts, k2.
Row 2 and every foll WS row: P.
Rows 11, 13, 15, 17 and 19: *K2, k2tog tbl, k2tog, k2, yfwd, k1, yfwd; rep from * to last 2 sts, k2.
Row 20: As row 2.
Rep last 20 rows to form patt.

Openwork rib
Cast on a multiple of 4 sts plus 1 st.
Row 1: K1, *k3, p1; rep from *.
Row 2: *K1, p3; rep from * to last st, p1.
Row 3: K1, *yfwd, sl 1, k2tog, psso, yfrn, p1; rep from *.
Row 4: As row 2.
Rep last 4 rows to form patt.

To finish
Weave in any loose yarn ends on 12 knitted patches, then lay out flat and gently press.
Thread ribbons and sequins through lace eyelets to embellish knits.
Patchwork top
Cut patches 27cm wide from fabrics A, B and C. Iron Staflex onto wrong side of each piece.
Sew together fabric patches into four panels, each 27cm wide by 123cm long, taking 1.5cm seams on fabric throughout.
Cut three strips of fabric A, each 11cm by 123cm. Then stitch three narrow strips to four pieced panels, alternating the widths.
Using microfilament thread, machine zigzag stitch three knitted pieces in random positions to each of four wide panels, stretching knitting to fit if necessary and leaving 1.5cm uncovered around outer edge of top for edging seam.
Patchwork backing
From A, cut four pieces each 50cm by 50cm; then from C, cut two pieces each 29cm by 50cm, and one strip 29cm by 123cm.
Iron Staflex to each backing piece.
Make two panels, each with two A squares sewn to either side of one C piece 29cm by 50cm.
Sew pieced panels to either side of strip in C to make a 123cm square.
With wrong sides together, place patchwork top on top of backing, pin and stitch around edges.
Patchwork edging
From assorted fabrics, cut 24 rectangles, each 10cm by 25cm.
Piece these rectangles together lengthways to make four long strips of six rectangles each. Trim two strips to 123cm and two to 130cm.
Press 1.5cm onto wrong side of one long edge of each strip.
With right sides together, and taking 1.5cm seams, stitch unpressed edge of two shorter edging strips to top and bottom of throw. Fold these strips over onto back of throw and slip stitch pressed edge to backing along stitching line.
Repeat this on other two edges, folding under raw edges at corners.

boudoir cushion

Pretty and pink! This is the perfect piece to adorn a favourite bedroom chair. It is knitted in smooth silky cotton yarn, and a simple stitch decorates the top and complements the frilled edging. Glass beads further embellish the skirt and satin bows tie the cushion prettily and practically in place.

boudoir cushion

materials

Any lightweight cotton-blend yarn, such as Debbie Bliss *Cathay*
   8 x 50g balls
Pair of 3.75mm knitting needles
3.75mm circular knitting needle for edging
Large blunt-ended yarn needle
35cm x 35cm feather-filled cushion pad
Approximately 500 small glass beads
Approximately 2.5m of satin ribbon, 5cm wide

size

One size, 35cm x 35cm

tension

22 sts and 30 rows to 10cm over stocking stitch using
   3.75mm needles

special abbreviations

make knot = p3tog leaving sts on left needle, then k same 3 sts tog,
  p them tog again and slip sts off left needle.

Knot pattern
Row 1 (RS): K.
Row 2 and every foll WS row: P.
Row 3: K1, * make knot, k3; rep from * to last 4 sts, make knot, k1.
Row 5: K.
Row 7: K4, * make knot, k3; rep from * to last st, k1.
Row 8: P.
Rep last 8 rows to form knot patt.

To make cushion top
Using 3.75mm needles, cast on 77 sts.
Beg with a k row, work 15 rows in st st, ending with WS facing for next row.
Next row (WS): P11, k55, p11.
Next row (RS): K11, p1, work row 1 of knot patt over next 53 sts, p1, k11.
Next row: P11, k1, work row 2 of knot patt over next 53 sts, k1, p11.
Cont with sts and knot patt as set until work measures 30cm from cast-on edge, ending with RS facing for next row.
Next row (RS): K11, p55, k11.
Beg with a p row, work 15 rows in st st.
Cast off.

To make cushion base
Using 3.75mm needles, cast on 77 sts.
Beg with a k row, work in st st for 35cm.
Cast off.

To make cushion edging
With RS of work facing and using 3.75mm needles, pick up and k 79 sts along cast-off edge of cushion top (back edge of cushion top).
Row 1 (WS): K4, *p1, k4; rep from * to end.
Row 2: P4, *m1, k1, m1, p4; rep from * to end.
Rows 3, 5 and 7: K4, *p3, k4; rep from * to end.
Rows 4 and 6: P4, *k3, p4; rep from * to end.
Row 8: P4, *[k1, m1 twice, k1, p4; rep from * to end.
Row 9: K4, *p5, k4; rep from * to end.
Row 10: P4, *k5, p4; rep from * to end.
Rows 11–18: Rep rows 9 and 10 four times.
Row 19: As row 9.
Row 20: P4, *k1, m1, k3, m1, k1, p4; rep from * to end.
Row 21: K4, *p7, k4; rep from * to end.
Row 22: P4, *k7, p4; rep from * to end.
Rows 23–30: Rep rows 21 and 22 four times.
Row 31: As row 21.

Work simple picot cast-off as foll:
Next row: Cast off 4 sts, * slip st on right needle back onto left needle, k twice into this st, cast off 4 sts; rep from * to end.
Work edging around remaining three sides of cushion as foll:
With RS of cushion top facing and using 3.75 circular needle, pick up and k 78 sts along one side edge of cushion, 78 sts along cast-on edge and 78 sts along remaining side edge of cushion. *234 sts.*
Work 31-row edging patt and picot cast-off on these sts.

To finish
Weave in any loose yarn ends.
Lay work out flat and gently steam.
Sew cushion base to top along three sides, using mattress stitch.
Insert cushion pad and sew final seam.
Cut ribbon into four pieces. Fold under one end of each piece to neaten and stitch a pair at each side of opening at back of cushion, under edging. Tie in a large bow.
Stitch a small glass bead to each point of picot edge.

tea-party tea cosy

materials

3m of 70cm wide tulle fabric, cut into a continuous strip (see below)
Pair of 9mm knitting needles
50cm of 70cm wide chinoiserie fabric and matching thread for lining
Shirring elastic
50cm of organza ribbon, 4cm wide

size

One size, approximately 43cm in circumference and 23cm tall

tension

12 sts and 20 rows to 10cm over garter stitch using 9mm needles

pattern notes

• To cut the tulle in a continuous strip of 'yarn', start by laying it out flat. Working from right to left, cut the tulle 2.5cm from the bottom edge to within 2cm of the left edge. Then cut from left to right 2.5cm away from the first cut, again leaving 2cm uncut at the right edge. Continue in this way, rolling the strip into a ball as you work.

To make tea cosy pieces (make 2)
Using 9mm needles, cast on 26 sts.
Work in garter st (k every row) for 23cm.
Cast off.

To finish
Using knitted pieces as templates, cut two pieces of lining fabric, allowing 1.5cm extra all around. Turn under edges on lining pieces and sew them to knitted pieces. With wrong sides together, sew seams, leaving gaps for spout and handle. Run a double line of shirring elastic through tulle knitting only, approximately 5cm down from top, and gently gather up. Make a floppy bow with organza ribbon and sew to cosy on gathered neck.

jacquard cushion

Inspired by boudoir wallpaper patterns, this petite cushion is knitted in two colours using the simple stranding technique. It is worked in mercerised cotton, backed in sumptuous velvet and trimmed with either braid or tassels.

jacquard cushion

materials

Any super-fine-weight mercerised cotton yarn, such as
  Yeoman *Cotton Cannele 4ply*
  A: 1 x 250g cone in black
  B: 1 x 250g in turquoise
Pair of 3.25mm knitting needles
Medium-size blunt-ended yarn needle
Approximately 50cm of black velvet fabric and matching sewing
  thread for cushion back
30cm x 30cm feather-filled cushion pad
1.3m of braid trim for edging (optional)

size

One size, approximately 30cm x 30cm

tension

29 sts and 36 rows to 10cm over pattern using 3.25mm needles

pattern notes

• For the reverse colourway, use A for B and B for A. The yarn
  amount specified is enough for both cushions.
• When working the stocking stitch colour pattern from the chart,
  read odd-numbered rows (knit rows) from right to left and even-
  numbered rows (purl rows) from left to right.
• Work the colour pattern using the stranding (Fair Isle) technique,
  stranding the yarn not in use loosely across the back of the work. Do
  not carry the yarn over more than three stitches at a time, but weave
  it under and over the colour being worked.

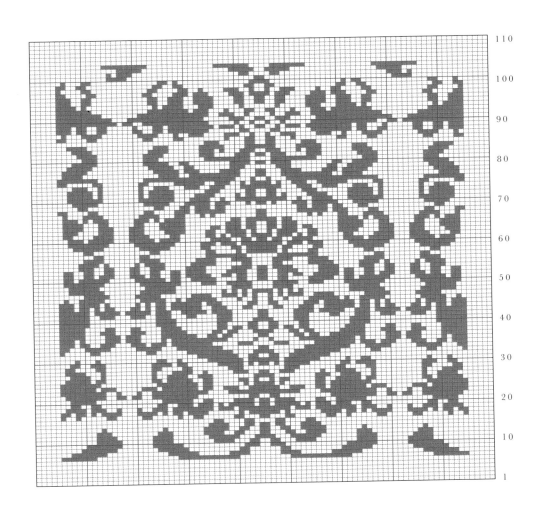

To make cushion front
Using 3.25mm needles and B, cast
on 90 sts.
Beg with a k row and chart row 1,
work 110 rows following chart.
Cast off.

To finish
Weave in any loose yarn ends.
Lay work out flat and gently steam.
For cushion back, cut two pieces of
fabric, each 27cm by 33cm.
Along one long edge of each piece
fold 1.5cm to wrong side twice and
stitch to form a double hem.
Lay knitting right-side up and place
both back pieces wrong-side up on
top, so that raw edges extend 1.5cm
past edges of knitting and hemmed
edges overlap at centre.
Pin and stitch around all sides,
taking a 1.5cm seam on fabric and
stitching close to edge on knitting.
Turn right-side out.

Tassels (optional)
Using a piece of cardboard 10cm
square and A, make four tassels in
same way as tassel on page 97, but
tying each tassel 2cm from top.
Sew one tassel to each corner
of cushion, or sew braid trim
around edge.
Insert cushion pad.

dress hangers

Make this special decorative hanger to display a vintage dress, as a gift for a bride or new homeowner, or simply to enjoy for your own use. Worked in two pieces, the knitted cover has a picot edge with knitted-in beads and sequins and random longer picots around the centre hook. The hook is covered in ribbon, which is then tied around the neck in a bow.

dress hanger

materials

Any super-fine-weight mercerised cotton yarn, such as
  Yeoman *Cotton Cannele 4ply*
  1 x 250g cone
Approximately 5m of ribbon, 7mm wide
Two pairs of 3.25mm knitting needles
Medium-size blunt-ended yarn needle
Approximately 100 assorted shiny sequins, glass seed beads and
  glass bugle beads
Standard-size padded and covered coat-hanger, approximately
  43cm long x 13cm around
Sewing needle and sewing thread to sew on extra beads and sequins

size

One size, to fit standard coat-hanger

tension

29 sts and 32 rows to 10cm over stocking stitch using 3.25mm needles

To make hanger cover

Using 3.25mm needles, cast on 124 sts.

Back of cover

Beg with a k row, work 19 rows in st st, ending with WS facing for next row.

Cut yarn leaving a long end, leave these sts on needle and set aside.

Front of cover

Thread approximately 60 beads and sequins onto yarn.

Using 3.25mm needles and yarn threaded with beads and sequins, cast on 124 sts.

Pushing beads and sequins along yarn (to use for picot cast-off) and beg with a k row, work 20 rows in st st, ending with RS facing for next row.

Do not cut yarn.

Join back and front

Join back and front of cover as foll:
Hold two needles with back and front on them in your left hand, the back behind the front with WS together and needle points facing to right, then with a third needle k to end of row, working 1 st from front needle tog with same st from needle behind. *124 sts.*

Picot cast-off

Remembering to transfer st on right needle to left needle after each cast-off, work picot cast-off as foll:
[Cast on 3 sts (onto left needle), insert bead/sequin, cast off next 6 sts] 19 times.

Cast on 26 sts, placing bead/sequin on each of last 4 sts, cast off next 28 sts.

Cast on 33 sts, placing bead/sequin on each of last 4 sts, cast off next 35 sts.

Cast on 44 sts, placing bead/sequin on each of last 4 sts, cast off next 46 sts.

Cast on 40 sts, placing bead/sequin on each of last 4 sts, cast off next 42 sts.

Cast on 20 sts, placing bead/sequin on each of last 4 sts, cast off next 22 sts.

[Cast on 3 sts, insert bead/sequin, cast off next 6 sts] 19 times.

Fasten off.

To finish

Weave in any loose yarn ends.

Lay work out flat and gently steam.

Sew seam on knitted cover, leaving one short end open.

Remove hook and push hanger into cover.

Sew short end closed.

Screw hook back into hanger, gently pushing through knitting.

Embellishments

Cover hook with satin ribbon by wrapping around hook in blanket-stitch fashion and secure with small sewing stitches.

Tie ribbon around neck of hook and tie in a bow. Sew a few sequins onto ribbon.

Embellish long tendrils randomly with beads and sequins to create pretty icicles.

knot stitch cushion

materials

Any super-fine-weight mercerised cotton yarn, such as
    Yeoman *Cotton Cannele 4ply*
    1 x 250g cone
Pair of 5mm knitting needles
Medium-size blunt-ended yarn needle
45cm x 45cm feather-filled cushion pad
50cm of silk fabric to cover cushion pad

size

One size, approximately 45cm x 45cm

tension

17 sts to 10cm over knot stitch pattern using 5mm needles

To make cushion front
Using 5mm needles, cast on 77 sts.
Beg with a k row, work 2 rows in
st st, ending with RS facing for
next row.
Beg knot stitch patt as foll:
Row 1 (RS): K3, *yfwd, sl 1, k2tog,
psso, yfwd, k1; rep from * to last
2 sts, k2.
Row 2: P.
Row 3: K2, k2tog, yfwd, k1,
*yfwd, sl 1, k2tog, psso, yfwd, k1;
rep from * to last 4 sts, yfwd, sl 1,
k1, psso, k2.

Row 4: P.
Rep last 4 rows until work measures
44cm from cast-on edge, ending
with RS facing for next row.
Beg with a k row, work 2 rows in
st st.
Cast off.

To make cushion back
Work exactly as for cushion front.

To finish
Weave in any loose yarn ends.
Lay work out flat and gently steam.

Cushion pad covering
Cut two pieces of fabric 48cm square.
With right sides together, stitch
around three sides, taking a 1.5cm
seam. Turn right-side out.
Insert cushion pad and slip stitch
opening closed.
Knitted cover
With wrong sides facing, sew three
seams of cushion cover, using
mattress stitch.
Insert cushion pad and sew last
seam.

key fob

This small project makes a great gift for a new homeowner. It consists of strands of knitted leaf motifs and I-cords with bobbles and is decorated with beads and stones, sequins, ribbon and a tassel to create an individual yet practical and pretty piece.

materials

Any super-fine-weight mercerised cotton yarn, such as
Yeoman *Cotton Cannele 4ply*
Pair of 2.75mm knitting needles
2 medium-size natural stone beads
2 large black irregular-shaped beads or stones
20cm of a strand of black sequins
20cm of very narrow black satin ribbon
50cm of taupe satin ribbon, 1cm wide
Snap hook

To make leaf shapes (make 2)
Using 2.75mm needles, cast on 3 sts
Row 1 (RS): K.
Row 2 and every foll WS row: P.
Row 3: [K1, m1] twice, k1.
Row 5: K2, m1, k1, m1, k2.
Row 7: K3, m1, k1, m1, k3.
Row 9: K4, m1, k1, m1, k4.
Row 11: K5, m1, k1, m1, k5. *13 sts.*
Row 13: Sl 1, k1, psso, k to last 2 sts, k2tog.
Row 15: As row 13.
Row 17: As row 13.
Row 19: As row 13.
Row 21: As row 13. *3 sts.*

Row 23: Sl 1, k2tog, psso.
Fasten off.
Make second leaf shape in same way.

I-cord with bobbles (make 2)
Using 2.75mm needles, cast on 1 st, leaving a long yarn end (to secure cord to snap hook).
Work this st in garter st (k every row) until cord measures 2cm.
Next row (bobble row) [K into front and back of st] twice, k into front of st again. *5 sts.*
K 1 row.

Next row P5tog. *1 st rem.*
Cont as set, working a bobble as before at random intervals between rows of garter st until cord measures approximately 7.5cm from cast-on edge.
Fasten off, leaving a long yarn end (to go through bead).
Make a second cord in same way approximately 11cm long.

To make tassel
Cut a piece of cardboard 13cm long (or length of tassel required) and wrap a generous amount of

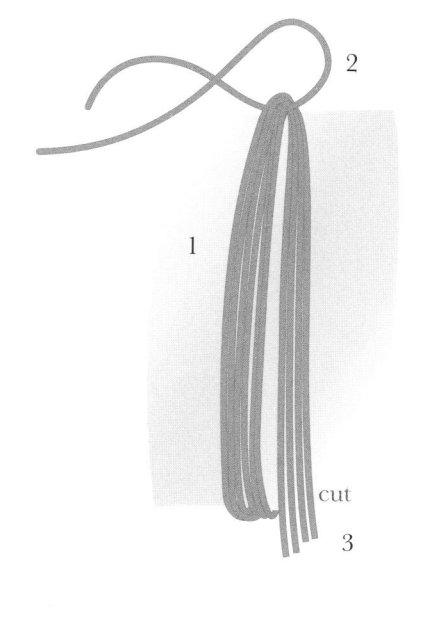

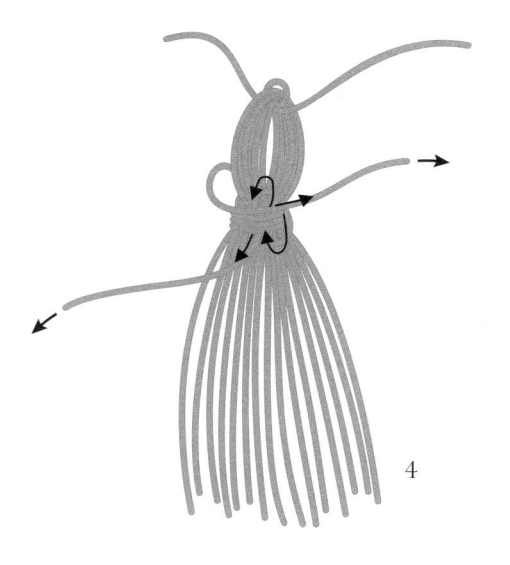

yarn around it.

Wrap a separate length of yarn a few times around strands at one end of cardboard and knot, leaving long enough loose ends for stitching tassel in place.

Cut strands at other end of tassel. Wrap another length of yarn around tassel, approximately 1.5cm from top (to form a 'neck'), linking and securing ends under wrapping.

To finish

Thread large 'item' bead onto longest length of I-cord and attach this cord to snap hook by folding over top and securing with a small stitch.

Thread smaller natural stone onto shorter length of I-cord and attach this cord to snap hook in same way. Next, attach lengths of sequins and narrow satin ribbon to snap hook in same way as cords.

Thread end at top of tassel through second 'item' bead, then through other natural stone. Attach tassel to snap hook with a knot and secure with a small stitch.

Sew two leaf shapes together around edges, fold top over snap hook and secure with a few small stitches.

Finally thread silk ribbon through the snap hook and tie in a bow.

pearl button and lace sequin cushions

These are the simplest of cushions, made in the most beautiful of yarns. For one, whisper-fine silk mohair in the palest pearl shade is embellished with natural mother-of-pearl buttons, randomly scattered for added glamour. To complement the first, the second cushion is worked in the same yarn, crafted into a delicate cobweb lace and scattered with silver sequins.

materials

pearl button cushion

Any fine-weight mohair-blend yarn, such as Rowan *Kidsilk Haze*
    4 x 25g balls
Pair of 3.75mm knitting needles
Approximately 70 mother-of-pearl buttons in assorted sizes

lace sequin cushion

Any fine-weight 4ply mohair-blend yarn, such as Rowan *Kidsilk Haze*
    2 x 25g balls
Pair of 5mm knitting needles
Approximately 100 small and medium silver shiny sequins
7 small mother-of-pearl buttons
50cm of 90cm wide silk fabric and matching sewing thread

both cushions

Medium-size blunt-ended yarn needle
Feather-filled cushion pad to fit finished cover

size

Pearl button cushion: One size, approximately 40cm x 40cm
Lace sequin cushion: One size, approximately 40cm x 30cm

tension

Pearl button cushion: 22 sts and 30 rows to 10cm over stocking
stitch using yarn double and 3.75mm needles
Lace sequin cushion: 19 sts and 24 rows to 10cm over stitch
    pattern using 5mm needles

stitches
lace stitch pattern

Row 1 (WS): K3, p to last 3 sts, k3.

Row 2: K5, *yfwd, k2, sl 1, k1, psso, k2tog, k2, yfwd, k1; rep from * to last 4 sts, k4.

Row 3: K3, p to last 3 sts, k3.

Row 4: K4, *yfwd, k2, sl 1, k1, psso, k2tog, k2, yfwd, k1; rep from * to last 5 sts, k5.

Rep last 4 rows to form lace stitch patt.

To make button cushion
Using 3.75mm needles and two strands of yarn held tog, cast on 81 sts.
Row 1 (RS): *K2, p1; rep from * to end.
Row 2: *K1, p2; rep from * to end.
Rep last 2 rib rows until work measures 2.5cm, ending with RS facing for next row.
Beg with a k row, work in st st until work measures 87.5cm from cast-on edge, ending with RS facing for next row.
Work in rib as for cast-on edge for 2.5cm.
Cast off in rib.

To make lace sequin cushion
Using 5mm needles, cast on 153 sts.

Work 2cm in lace stitch patt, ending with RS facing for next row.
Next row (buttonhole row): K1, yfwd, k2tog, patt to end.
Cont in patt and work 6 more buttonholes approximately 4cm apart **and at the same time** cont until work measures 30cm from cast-on edge, ending with WS facing for next row.
Cast off.

To finish both cushions
Weave in any loose yarn ends.
Lay work out flat and gently steam.
Button cushion
Fold edges into centre, overlapping by 5cm.
Sew side seams with mattress stitch, working through all layers.

Scatter buttons randomly over cushion front and sew in place.
Insert cushion pad.
Lace cushion
Fold edges into centre, overlapping by width of garter stitch borders.
Sew side seams with mattress stitch, working through all layers.
Scatter sequins randomly over cushion front and sew in place.
Sew on buttons to match buttonholes.
For fabric cushion pad cover, cut two pieces of silk fabric, each 43cm square. With right sides of fabric together, stitch around three sides, taking a 1.5cm seam. Turn right-side out.
Insert cushion pad, slip stitch seam closed and insert in lace cover.

yarns

Although I have recommended specific yarns for the projects in the book, you can use substitutes if you like. A description of each of the yarns used is given below.

If you decide to use an alternative yarn, purchase a substitute yarn that is as close as possible to the original in thickness, weight and texture so that it will work with the pattern instructions. Buy only one ball to start with, so you can test the effect. Calculate the number of balls you will need by meterage rather than by weight. The recommended knitting-needle size and knitting tension on the ball bands are extra guides to the yarn thickness.

To obtain Debbie Bliss, Rowan (and Jaeger) or Yeoman yarns, go to the websites below to find a mail-order stockist or store in your area:

www.debbieblissonline.com
www.knitrowan.com
www.yeoman-yarns.co.uk

Debbie Bliss *Cathay*
A lightweight cotton-blend yarn
Recommended knitting-needle size: 3.75mm
Tension: 22 sts x 30 rows per 10cm over knitted st st
Ball size: 100m per 50g ball
Yarn specification: 50% cotton, 35% viscose microfibre, 15% silk

Debbie Bliss *Pure Silk*
A double-knitting-weight silk yarn
Recommended knitting-needle size: 4mm
Tension: 24 sts x 30 rows per 10cm over knitted st st
Hank size: 125m per 50g ball
Yarn specification: 100% pure silk

Jaeger *Siena*
A super-fine-weight mercerised cotton yarn
Recommended knitting-needle size: 2.75–3mm
Tension: 28 sts x 38 rows per 10cm over knitted st st
Ball size: 140m per 50g ball
Yarn specification: 100% mercerised cotton

Jaeger *Silk 4ply*
A super-fine-weight silk yarn
Recommended knitting-needle size: 3mm
Tension: 28 sts x 38 rows per 10cm over knitted st st
Ball size: 186m per 50g ball
Yarn specification: 100% silk

Rowan *Cotton Glacé*
A fine-weight cotton yarn
Recommended knitting-needle size: 3.25–3.75mm
Tension: 23 sts x 32 rows per 10cm over knitted st st
Ball size: 115m per 50g ball
Yarn specification: 100% cotton

Rowan *Kidsilk Haze*
A fine-weight mohair-blend yarn
Recommended knitting-needle size: 3.25–5mm
Tension: 18–25 sts x 23–24 rows per 10cm over knitted st st
Ball size: 210m per 25g ball
Yarn specification: 70% super kid mohair, 30% silk

Rowan *Lurex Shimmer*
A super-fine-weight metallic-mix yarn
Recommended knitting-needle size: 3.25mm
Tension: 29 sts x 41 rows per 10cm over knitted st st
Ball size: 95m per 25g ball
Yarn specification: 80% viscose, 20% polyester

Rowan *RYC Luxury Cotton DK*
A double-knitting weight cotton-blend yarn
Recommended knitting-needle size: 4mm
Tension: 22 sts x 30 rows per 10cm over knitted st st
Ball size: 95m per 50g ball
Yarn specification: 50% cotton, 45% viscose, 5% silk

Yeoman *Cotton Cannele 4ply*
A super-fine-weight mercerised cotton yarn
Recommended knitting-needle size: 2.75mm
Tension: 33 sts x 44 rows per 10cm over knitted st st
Cone size: 875m per 250g cone
Yarn specification: 100% mercerised cotton